Can You See the Signs

Denise Fenstermaker

Copyright (c) 2016 Denise Fenstermaker.

All rights reserved. No part(s) of this book may be reproduced, distributed or transmitted in any form, or by any means, or stored in a database or retrieval systems without prior expressed written permission of the Author of this book.

ISBN: 978-1-62217-581-9

*I dedicate this book to the survivors of domestic violence
and to the ones who didn't survive.*

*To the survivors: you're free to live and love life again. To the ones
who didn't survive: you're still loved and missed by many.*

*Although domestic violence is not gender-specific,
I wrote this book from a female perspective.*

*In each of the stories in this book,
the names have been changed to protect the innocent.*

Contents

Prologue: Can You See the Signs 1

1. Warning Signs 3

Elaine's Story 11

2. Once You're In—How to Get Out 17

Diane's Story 21

3. Be Safe—Stay Alive 26

Shona's Story 28

4. You're Stronger Than You Think—Don't Give Up 35

Stephanie's Story 39

5. This Is Not What We're Made For — What We Know
About How to Treat Each Other 43

Christy's Story 49

6. Recovery Takes Time and Help 55

Teresa's Story 60

7. What About the Children? How Does it Affect Them? 65

Suzanne's Story 70

8. Where to Go for Help—Your Legal Rights 75

Kelly's Story 78

9. Practice Personal Safety 83

Karen's Story 86

10. Pam's Story 89

Thank You 92

About the Author 94

Prologue

Can You See the Signs

Being isolated and lonely is a way of life when you're in an abusive relationship. You try to minimize your abuse. You say to yourself: "It's not that bad. He didn't really mean to hurt me, he just had a bad day. It will be different as soon as…" Those will become the phrases that keep you in the relationship. "That's it, I'm leaving": how many times do we say that to ourselves?

Months turn to years and we're still there. Our pride has vanished; our self-esteem has been gone so long we forgot we ever had any. Days and nights come and go like a blur. Am I alive or just existing? Every day you put on a painted face. You smile and say, "I'm fine, how are you?" Some people never notice that you're living a double life. Some people actually think you're happy. They don't know that inside you feel like you're being eaten away by despair. You feel like a fool. How could you let someone treat you like this? I used to be a strong person—what happened? Does all this sound familiar?

Can You See the Signs

I hope and pray that this book is a blessing that helps the victims realize they're not alone and that it educates others about domestic violence. Abuse doesn't have to be a way of life.

> *Remember, every flower that ever bloomed had to go through dirt to get there.*
> — Rainer Maria Rilke

> *Dreams are renewable. No matter what our age or condition, there are still untapped possibilities within us and new beauty waiting to be born.*
> — Dale E. Turner

> *We do not understand:*
> *Joy until we face sorrow.*
> *Faith until it's been tested.*
> *Peace until faced with conflict.*
> *Trust until we are betrayed.*
> *Love until it is lost.*
> *Hope until confronted with doubt.*
> — Author unknown

Chapter One

WARNING SIGNS

1: Intimidation

About People:

- An abuser may look angry at you for smiling at the waiter at a restaurant.
- An abuser may look hard at you and breathe hard where you can hear him so that you know he's angry or upset with you. You might have laughed at a man's joke or agreed with something someone said.
- An abuser may get angry because you remembered someone from high school and were able to call that person by name. It might be a childhood friend or a schoolmate you had a crush on.
- About Animals:
- An abuser may kick or hit an animal, pull their tails or do other cruel things to them. Some have tied things to their tails that they can't get free from; some have even burned

them. The abuser usually feels no regret or remorse for the pain they have caused that pet.
- An abuser may say the animal can't have food or water even though it is tied and cannot care for itself. He may also not allow shelter for this pet and not allow you to do anything to help it.
- An abuser may be jealous of your pet and choke, stab or shoot the pet to death so that it can no longer get in the way of receiving your attention.

With Weapons:

- An abuser may sit and sharpen knives and look at you to scare you and not say a word.
- An abuser may clean a gun or just hold it and say things like: "Don't make me have to use this" or "I wonder if I could hit you from here."
- An abuser may display weapons and describe what he could do to you with each one.

2: Emotional Abuse

Belittling:

- An abuser may tell the victim that she couldn't make it without him because she's too dumb.
- The abuser may make fun of the way the victim talks, especially if the victim has a speech impediment.

- An abuser may tell the victim that no one would want them her because of skin texture, freckles, or scars.

Name-Calling:

- An abuser may call the victim an ugly name in front of other people, then laugh and say, "You know I'm just picking. Don't be so sensitive," and then have no regret for hurting and embarrassing the victim.
- A victim is called names to belittle her on a regular basis, such as: bitch, whore, slut, pig, etc.
- An abuser may wake up cussing at the victim because the abuser didn't sleep well and says it's the victim's fault.

Jealousy:

- At the beginning of a relationship, an abuser may say that jealously is good because it shows the abuser loves the victim.
- A victim may be accused of flirting with the bag boy at the grocery store, a gas station, or a restaurant. The victim usually feels safer by staring at the floor so the abuser cannot have any reason to be upset about where she is looking.

Control:

- An abuser will sometimes tell you that he will take the child or children and you'll never see them again. The abuser

will sometimes hurt the children physically, verbally, or emotionally to cause pain to you.
- Abusive people have unrealistic expectations. They expect a perfect wife, mother, lover, and friend, one who takes care of all his needs and desires.
- Abusers want control at all times, even to the point of deciding what the victim eats, how long she will be in the bath or shower, as well as when and how long she sleeps.
- An abuser will often escort the victim to and from work, shopping, hair appointments, doctor appointments, etc. An abuser may demand that the victim check in frequently by phone, pager, cell phone or text message.
- Abusers are known to follow their victims if they let them go anywhere alone.
- Abusers are known to isolate their victims by moving to isolated areas, not letting her drive the car, or not letting her work or go to school. They also keep them from visiting family and friends.
- The silent treatment is another form of emotional abuse. It is used by the abuser to keep the victim stressed because she doesn't know what the abuser is going to do next.
- An abuser often times wants the victim to look unattractive by encouraging her to overeat, to not fix her hair, and to not wear any make-up.
- An abuser may threaten to commit suicide, or put a gun to their own head or a knife to their own wrist, or even take some pills just to try to keep and control her.

3: Destroying Property

- The abuser will commonly hit doors, walls, tables, etc. in order to scare the victim into submission.
- Abusers have no respect for their partners or belongings. An abuser might break something that means a lot to their victim. Sometimes they tear or burn pictures of loved ones just to gain control over the victim. Sometimes they destroy furniture by breaking or burning it to try and gain dominance over their victim.

4: Physical Abuse

- Abusers will use different tactics to try to control their victims, such as pinching, hitting, slapping with an open hand, or punching with a closed fist.
- More signs of physical abuse are being pushed or held (restrained) against the floor, wall, door, couch, bed, ground, etc.
- Preventing their partner from leaving a room, home, car, or any other area is physical abuse.
- Abusers have choked their victims with their hands or other objects like extension cords and telephone cords until they were unconscious or dead.
- Abusers often throw objects at their partner or hit their partner with things such as telephones, ashtrays, furniture or whatever they can get their hands on. This is another pathetic way of trying to beat them into submission.

- There have been lots of cases where knives and guns have been used to force the victim to do something or to cause harm to that person. Example: Abusers have put a knife or gun to their partner's throat or head in order to put fear in the victim, to control them, but never hurt them.
- Some abusers have cut their victims just enough to make them bleed, but not enough to need stitches, to try to gain the control they desire.
- Some abusers have put an unloaded gun to the victim's head and pulled the trigger so the abuser can get the reaction they want, without the innocent victim knowing the gun is empty.
- Some abusers have burned their victims with cigarettes, lighters, candles, irons, torches, and curling irons to try and break the will of their victim.
- Abusers have also used hot liquids such as hot coffee, hot tea, candle wax, etc. to torment their partner.

All of these things are physical abuse.

5: Sexual Abuse

- Abusers may force their partners to have sex, or forcefully tell their partners that they will have sex with them even if the victim doesn't want to.
- The victim may be sick, tired, stressed, or recovering from some type of illness or surgery, but the abuser has no compassion for the victim. The abuser only thinks of himself.

Warning Signs

- Abusers may force their partners to have oral or anal sex as a way of controlling them. They also may use objects to sexually abuse their partner in order to appease their demented desires.
- Some abusers force their partner to watch pornographic movies and look at pornographic magazines or books. The abuser may want to act out what they see on their victims. It might be with whips, chains, restraints, or some type of pain that is administered during sex.
- Some abusers treat their victims as sex objects. Some have put their partner in a collar and leash and had them act like a dog. Some want their victim to sit at their feet like a good dog until sex is wanted again.
- Abusers have forced their partners to allow pictures to be taken of them in sexual positions and then have posted them on the Internet.
- Some abusers have some kind of signal that means it is time for sex. The victim is supposed to respond willingly or suffer consequences.
- Abusers have used their victims as prostitutes and sold them to their friends and family members.
- Abusers will often expect their victims to have sex after an abusive episode as a way of "making up." They may think it relieves any responsibility of guilt. The abuser may think that after sex everything is okay and the victim should act as if there's nothing wrong.

6: Financial Abuse

- The abuser may control all the money. This person may be the one that handles the checkbook, writes out the bills and insists that he can do it better.
- Abusers often make all the big financial decisions and most small ones. Example: buying a house, a car, a boat, or other entertainment vehicles. They don't discuss any aspect of it with their partner until the decision is final.
- The abuser will usually keep tabs on all money. They expect their partner to explain where any money was spent. A lot of times abusers won't allow their victims to have any money, and if they give the victim money, they want to see receipts for money spent.

Elaine's Story

I LIVED IN AN APARTMENT and there was a party going on below me. My neighbors invited me to come. It was silly, but another girl and I were in competition to see who could get Doug's attention. He had lots of tattoos and piercings and I was intrigued. I woke up the next morning with him in my bed. He had never left from the night before. I was nineteen years old. I was with him a year and a half. He was a lot bigger than me. He was 6'2" and weighed over 260 pounds. I am 5'2" and weigh 118 pounds. I was high-strung, headstrong, and wasn't going to let anybody tell me what I could and couldn't do.

The abuse started one night when he told me I couldn't go anywhere. I was in the bedroom and he blocked the door. I kneed him in the crotch, hit him in the stomach and then stepped over him and went to see my grandma like I had told him I wanted to to begin with. I came home later and was sitting in a rocking chair. He reached down and flipped me out of the chair. We started fighting and ended up in the bathroom. He knocked me into the tub and was trying to stomp my head, so I put my arm up and he stomped my arm until he broke it. Doug never worked but he would take my money and car and go party and cheat with other women.

He had kids by two other women. I found out later that he abused them too. The first ex-wife moved on, got married, and had more kids, but the second ex-wife would cause arguments because she didn't want her child around my child because my child is biracial. My child stayed with my grandmother a lot but knew about the abuse.

Doug cheated on me with his second ex-wife. She didn't learn her lesson until she found out what he did to me.

I was a dancer and I worked seven days a week. We moved from the apartment into a house when I found out I was pregnant. To cover up for his drugs, drinking, and other women, he would start fights with me for no reason. Then he would take my car and leave. He didn't have a driver's license. Each time he would come back, cry, and tell me that it wasn't my fault, it was his. He had a really bad childhood, and I thought if I showed him enough love that he would be okay.

I was working and going to school so I decided to quit school so he could go. That didn't last long. He quit too. I was really sick with my pregnancy, so I decided to go and stay with my grandmother. Since Doug was okay with that, I should have realized something was wrong. I got to my grandmother's and realized that I had forgotten my medicine, so I went back to the house and Doug's second ex-wife answered the door in my gown. I got mad and started cussing and arguing with her. Doug came out, grabbed me by my throat, and picked me up in the air. His ex-wife told him to put me down because I was pregnant. He put me down and I called my grandmother. My grandmother came down and called the police and he was arrested.

When he got out of jail, he moved in with his grandmother. His grandmother was very sick, so I moved in too to help take care of her. Things got really bad then. He locked me in the bedroom for days. I had no food, and had to use the bathroom in a trash can. His grandmother let me out one day when he was gone. Another day I was at the kitchen table taking care of his grandmother and he said he wanted to go out. I told him that he couldn't use my car, so he punched me in the side of the head. There was another incident when I told him that I was leaving, and he got me in the bathroom and was kicking and hitting me, so I cowered down to cover my stomach to protect my baby. He grabbed me by the hair and slammed my face into the toilet seat, which broke my jaw.

I finally decided I couldn't take his abuse any more. I had goals, and things I wanted to do with my kids. Doug tried to stop me, but my other grandmother was there. She was a big lady, so I got my stuff and headed out the door. I saw Doug trying to hit my grandmother with a flashlight through the passenger-side window. I jumped on Doug's back, fat belly and all, and he slung me across the trunk of the car. My grandmother got out of the car and was coming after Doug. I got in between them and told my grandma we just needed to leave. I took out restraining orders at different times, but by the time we went to court I would drop them because he would threaten to kill my grandparents, my kids, or me if I didn't drop them. I went into labor and Doug came to the hospital. He cut the cord, but he got mad when I wouldn't give my child his last name. We got into an argument and he threw an orange juice bottle at me while I was nursing the baby. I left the hospital with my grandmother.

The night before Doug tried to kill me, he had been following me. I was scared, but I pulled over at a store. He said he wanted to see us, so I told him that he could follow us to my grandmother's house. That was going well until he ripped his pants while teasing and playing with us. I told him to take them off and I would sew them up. Doug tried to rape me while we were in the bedroom, so I dragged the needle down his face. My grandmother came in and told him to leave.

The next day I had to go to work. Doug called and said that he had forgotten to give the kids their Christmas presents the night before. He wanted to meet me and give them to me. I knew if I didn't that he would come to my job and cause trouble or get me fired. I met him in a parking lot. I had the doors locked and the window rolled down just enough to reach for the presents. He told me that he'd gotten me something too. He said it wasn't much but it was from the heart. He told me to close my eyes and he would give me my gift. He managed to get his hand through the window and unlocked the door. When I opened my eyes, he had a knife to my stomach. He told me that if I ever wanted to see the kids again, I had to do what he said. I was trying to reason with him and trying to get the knife away from him at the same time. He stabbed me several times. The blade broke off and I threw it out the window. My hand was cut and he still had the handle. He pushed me into the passenger seat and was hitting me. I had long hair, and he twisted it and stuck it under his leg. He told me to change the gears while he drove. Doug didn't live far from where we were, and I kept telling him to think about what he was doing. I told him that he would never see the kids again if he killed me. I kept knocking the car out of gear with my elbow. He punched me in the face so many times that he broke all the bones around my eye. He split both my lips to the gums. I knew he was going to kill me so I thought, "Okay, we'll both die."

Right before I did anything else, I prayed to God that He wouldn't let my kids grow up without their mom like I did. My mom died when I was twelve. I grabbed the steering wheel, and the car went off the road and flipped. It landed in a field. I could hardly see, but I thought, "If I can get out, I'm going to run." As I was getting one leg out, Doug grabbed the other one and stabbed me in the back of my leg. He had gotten another knife from somewhere. I fell out into the field, and Doug came out on top of me. I don't remember what he was saying but I saw a bright light and I felt at peace. I saw my mom and she told me that it wasn't my time to go, and I needed to go back.

I came to and Doug was gone. I crawled back to the car, trying to feel my way around because I couldn't see from the blood and broken bones. I was looking for a cigarette and a cell phone when someone knocked on the window and asked if I was the only one out there. At that point, Doug had run because he thought he had killed me. When I fell unconscious, he had cut my face and throat, and stabbed me in the back of my neck. I told the police that I wouldn't tell them anything until I knew my kids were safe. I knew they were with my grandmother. The police found my kids and brought them to the hospital. The doctor called the family in because they didn't think I was going to make it. I told the police who did this to me, but Doug had already bragged to someone that he had killed me, so they'd called the police too. He was sentenced to a little over eleven years in prison, and I still fear for my life and the lives of my kids and family. My children have obviously been affected by all this; but I'm thankful that God answered my prayer, and I get to be here for them. I had to have 496 stitches in my face and neck alone, and have several other things I deal with because of what he did to me. If I could say one thing to help someone that's being abused it would be to go with your gut, not your heart. Don't stay and put yourself through it.

> *When a man is wrapped up in himself,*
> *he makes a pretty small package.*
> — John Ruskin

> *Courage is fear that has said its prayers.*
> — Joyce Meyer

Chapter Two

Once You're In—How to Get Out

People don't get into abusive relationships on purpose. A lot of times the abuser starts out so wonderful and charming: a dream-come-true kind of guy, your knight in shining armor. Then, days, weeks, and months into the relationship, the abuse begins. It might start out with isolation from your friends and family in such a kind way. He says he just wants to spend cherished moments with you. The abuser has a habit of making plans for a get-away when family and friends' events are already in place.

A bad temper soon turns into a slap across the face. An apology follows later, along with, "If you had done different, this wouldn't have happened." You start thinking: "What did I do and what can I do so it doesn't happen again?" Things get broken and keepsakes are destroyed. You hear, "I'm sorry, it won't happen again." The abuser uses excuses; I'm under pressure, it's because of my job, I'm stressed, it's one excuse after another. Now I ask you: can you see the signs?

Let others know what's going on and what your plans are so they can help you escape to a safe place.

Any amount of money you can save will help. Change turns to cash. Don't risk getting caught hiding it. Keep it in a safe place. If you work, take it there, even if you have to hide it in your shoe. If you don't work then hide it somewhere he wouldn't normally look such as: in a sock behind the dryer, behind a dresser, or in a basement somewhere, or even the attic.

Try to buy or get someone to buy some phone cards or a cell phone. Don't make any arrangements to leave via your home phone if you can help it. The phone may be bugged.

Make an escape plan. Write it down, then hide it. Tape it to the bottom of a drawer, or hide it on top of duct work in the basement or attic, inside a clock, inside a toy, or behind a picture in a frame. Put it anywhere your abuser won't find it. This is for your protection. If your abuser finds this, it could delay your escape or cause more abuse.

Don't tell your child about the escape ahead of time. Some children might not want to leave. A child might get scared and go and tell the abuser what the plan is. The child might not understand that this is not a way of life. A lot of children have been exposed to abusive situations since the day they were born.

If possible, remove any treasured items before your escape—only if you can do it without your abuser finding out. Once you're out, don't look back. Just get somewhere safe. Once you're out, you might think about something you wish you had gotten. Leave it. Remember: it could cost you your life or the life of your child. It's not worth dying for.

Once You're In—How to Get Out

Here Are Some Things You Want to Get / Copy Before You Leave:

- driver's license / some type of picture ID
- birth certificates
- money
- lease, rental agreement, deed for the house, and / house or rent payment book
- bank books
- check books
- credit cards
- insurance papers
- keys to the house, cars, and office
- any medicine you or your children might need
- any small items that can be sold
- address book
- pictures
- family medical records
- social security cards
- TANF/ WIC /FOOD STAMP paperwork
- school records
- work permits
- green card
- passports
- marriage certificate
- divorce papers
- jewelry
- children's favorite toys and blankets

Can You See the Signs

Please remember: these things can be replaced, and even if they can't be, don't worry about it. Your and your child's lives can't be replaced. Don't risk it. Your family and friends could help you hide some things. A co-worker or a trusted doctor of yours or your children might be willing to keep some things in a safe place until you can get them.

Diane's Story

I MET JACK AT WORK. We had an affair. I left my husband, he left his wife, and we moved in together. It wasn't long before the abuse started. I was filled with so much guilt that Jack used that to start to control me and beat me down emotionally. I knew I had made a bad mistake by leaving my husband but I thought it was too late to go back.

Jack didn't drink, do drugs, or even smoke. He was just evil. When Jack started calling me names and putting me down, I felt like I deserved whatever I got because of leaving my husband. He acted like I could tell him anything about my past. He asked lots of questions. Little did I know that everything I said would be thrown up in my face later.

At first the abuse was name-calling and criticizing the way I dressed, my jewelry, and everything I had done in the past. Jack burnt my clothes, jackets, coats, boots, bras, panties, and anything I had worn before I married him. We drove through town and I had to tell him about any restaurant I had eaten at with my ex-husband. Jack said we'd never eat at any of those places. He kept me away from my family and friends. I was never allowed to be by myself. We worked at the same place so he would call my pager over a dozen times a day just to ask what I was doing, who was I talking to, and where I was. He would ask where I was, and not long after he would show up there. I wasn't supposed to talk to any other man or even say good morning.

I got pregnant before we were married and Jack convinced me that I didn't want to have the baby. He said I would hate myself if I had a bastard child. Having that abortion is a decision that I will regret forever. Both of his kids came to live with us shortly after we moved in together. If I was sick, he would make one of the kids stay home to keep an eye on me. We had new vehicles and we traveled a lot, so people thought we were a great couple that got along really well. Every day wasn't bad, but there were more bad days than good. We lived in four different homes in the six years we were together. We also bought at least six different vehicles, of which only one was used. Jack liked for people to think that we had a lot of money. The only time we got along well was when we were building something or buying something. I lost who I was.

I kept thinking that things would get better, after we got married, or after we got a certain home, car, or whatever. It never did. I learned quickly that going against the grain only made for all-night fights. I've never seen a man who could go without sleep like he could. Jack would jerk the covers off of me in the middle of the night, shake me, get up in my face, and ask if I was asleep. Sometimes he would take all the covers and tell me that I didn't need any. I would sleep in sweatpants, a sweatshirt, and socks. Jack would go through my pocketbook when I was in the shower. If I was in the shower too long, Jack would either throw my clothes in

Diane's Story

the shower, or turn the main water off to the house so I couldn't finish bathing. Jack broke over five hundred worth of collectables. He got mad several times and, while holding me by the throat or shoulders, he would head-butt me. He wouldn't let me use mouthwash because he said only whores used mouthwash.

Jack would buy me gifts to try to make up for whatever he had done to me, or he'd want to go out to eat or make travel plans because of his guilt. I felt like I couldn't think for myself. I had no self-esteem left. I felt worthless, and I got to the point that I didn't even care if he killed me. He picked out the clothes and shoes he wanted me to wear. They were things that I would never have picked out for myself. I wanted to go to the funeral of a friend of my family, so Jack said he'd take time off from work and go with me. Instead, he drove to the mountains and kept driving around until he knew the funeral was over. He knew what that lady meant to me, but it didn't matter.

I got pregnant again while I was taking birth control pills. I knew that no matter what, I wasn't going to kill this baby. Jack would have to kill me first. I told him that I had not started my monthly period. He said, "You better not be pregnant." The next day I found out I was. I was scared, happy, terrified, and stressed. Jack accused me of cheating on him, which was a joke because I wasn't even allowed to go to the grocery store by myself. Jack was mad, and said that he just about had his two kids raised, and he didn't want to raise any more. I told him that he didn't have to help raise our child, that I could do it myself. There were lots of times that I fought back, but I just ended up with more bruises. He told me that he was a third-degree black belt, and that he could kill me and never leave a mark on me. I had an unborn child to fight for now, and I wasn't going to let this one go. Jack tried several times to get me to miscarry. He tried jumping on my stomach, scaring me during the night and keeping me from sleep. Jack weighed 215 pounds. One night while I was asleep, Jack sat on me. Then he put a pillow over my face and tried to suffocate me. I thought I was going to die. I tried to think quickly; if I held my breath and relaxed, he would think I was dead and get off me. It worked.

I took an eight-week leave when I had my baby. I didn't know it at first, but Jack had bugged the phone. He started repeating things I'd said to my mom or to a friend. When Jack was at work, I'd call my mom or a friend. They knew something was terribly wrong with the man I had married. I left him three times. Jack would call repeatedly and swear he'd get psychological help, and that he'd never do it again. I'd go back because I hated letting him have visitation with our son. I was scared that he would hurt or kill my baby. Before long, it would start again. The final time he punched me was in front of our child and the baby started screaming and reaching for me. Jack wouldn't let me have him. I knew then that I wasn't going to put my child through this anymore. I left for good.

It's been a hard road, but it's been worth it in order to have peace. I had to let Jack have rights to see my baby. That has been the hard part. My child went through three years of therapy because of the stress of what he saw. From age three to six years old. That was a great help. If I could say one thing to someone that is in an abusive situation, it would be: it's not your fault and that you can't change them. Plan, prepare, and run!

Never confuse a single defeat for a finale defeat.
— F. Scott Fitzgerald

The journey of a thousand miles must begin with a single step.
— Lao Tzu

The 3 L's: Live Well, Laugh Often, Love Much.
— Author unknown

Chapter 3

Be Safe—Stay Alive

Increasing your safety on a day-to-day or moment-by-moment routine is a must. Knowing the areas that are danger zones could save your life. Avoid bathrooms, kitchens, and garages if at all possible. There are too many things that could be used as weapons. Try to hide sharp objects so they will be out of sight when the violence occurs. An abuser might strike out with a knife if an argument starts in the kitchen. Garages need to be avoided if possible because of shovels, sharp tools, chemicals, and gas that can be used by the abuser to harm or kill their victim.

Be careful when taking a bath. A shower would be safer. In a bathtub, you could be vulnerable to being held under the water or the abuser could throw something in the bathtub to electrocute you.

Be careful about what you eat or drink, when it has been prepared by your abuser. It is easy to dissolve chemicals, drugs, and poison in food and drinks. Be aware of strange flavors or colors that aren't normal. If you should get sick after you eat or drink something, somehow let someone know what you've had. Get professional help

Be Safe—Stay Alive

as soon as possible. If you take medicine in capsules, be careful not to leave it where it could be easily tampered with.

Be careful around candles, and in the kitchen around the stove. An abuser might use hot wax or the burner on the stove to cause pain to the victim so they will submit to whatever the abuser might want at the time.

Red flag: be careful if your abuser wants to take out an insurance policy on you, or up the value of the one you currently have, especially if he doesn't feel the need to have one on him, or to change the one he has. Some abusers plan the death of their victims because they don't want to let them go.

Red flag: if your abuser wants the two of you to take a hike in the mountains or take a cruise alone, be sure to let someone know where you're going, if possible. If your abuser has a history of abuse, always be suspicious of any surprise getaway for two. It could be the last time you're seen alive.

Stay alert, stay safe, stay alive.

Shona's Story

Tim and I met through church. I was a twenty-six-year-old single mother of three, trying to make a life for me and my kids.

Tim messaged me on Facebook. I would give him one-word comments or just say, "See you at church." He tried for three months to get me to talk to him at length. One day at church he came up and introduced himself to me. For about a month after that, he would come out to the church playground and talk to me while I pushed the kids on the swings. I saw his Facebook profile and didn't really care for all the sexy pictures of himself. He did act like a Christian though. He was community-oriented and was all about family. The first couple of times we went out were on group dates. Then we started going out on our own. We dated for about three months when the abuse started.

It was verbal abuse to begin with. We were at a restaurant, eating, and he got a call. He started cussing to the person on the phone, which I thought was odd because I had never heard him talk that way before.

I said, "Tim," and gave him a surprised look.

He said, "Shut the fuck up and don't you ever correct me again."

Shona's Story

I said, "I want to go home."

Tim started apologizing. He said he couldn't believe those words came out of his mouth. At the time, he was very believable.

The bad attitude and cussing came more often. After we had been dating five months or so, Tim confessed that he smoked dope and needed help. I was willing to help him any way I could.

It was probably a month after that when we were driving down the highway and he asked me about a guy I had dated before I met him. I told him the truth because I had no reason to lie. He spat in my face and started calling me all kinds of bad names. He tried to backhand me in the face, but I ducked and he hit me in the head. I said I wanted to get out so he slammed on the brakes and I flew forward. Then he started going fast again. He was going about seventy miles per hour from what I could see and then he reached over, unbuckled my seatbelt and said he wasn't going to stop but that I could jump. He kept calling me names.

When we got to a stop light, I tried to get out but he grabbed my hair and yanked me back in the car. He held me by my hair until we got to his house. He grabbed me by the neck and was dragging me to the house. I was screaming but the neighbors that were outside didn't do anything. I tried holding on to the doorframe of the house but that didn't work.

He got me into the house. He started punching the walls and then punching himself. He was going from anger to crying. He picked up a fire poker and started hitting the wall around me. He fell in a corner and was saying that I ruined his life.

I said "How?"

"You didn't tell me about everybody you had dated."

I started to leave and he pulled a small gun from a box and put it to his head. I stayed and talked to him so he would put the gun down. Tim's parents called and asked me to come over and talk to them. They said that Tim was bipolar and was off his medication. We broke up.

Tim would come to church or by my house and act real sweet. My kids thought he was great because he would buy them gifts, and get on the floor and play with them. He was on good behavior around them.

Although we weren't dating anymore, I let him call me and talk about his issues and about his childhood. Before long, he would start on me, saying he knew why my husband left me and that I was a terrible mother. He knew what to say to break me down. I hung up on him and ignored his calls. He called my work the next day and called my cell phone over a hundred times.

A day or two later, Tim showed up at my door. I didn't answer. He was banging on the door and trying to talk me into opening it.

I was on the phone with Joe, a friend of mine. Joe said, "Hang up and call the police, I'm on my way." So I did. As soon as I got the police on the phone, Tim broke down the door. He had already kicked in the garage door trying to find a way into the house. I started to run into the other room but Tim caught me by my ponytail. He lifted me up by my hair and slammed me on the tile floor. I almost passed out.

Tim said, "If you don't want the kids to see anything, then you had better listen to me."

I stayed quiet but thought about the last time he had been to the house in a rage. That time he bent me backwards by pulling my hair and trying to force my face under the faucet in the kitchen. I still have back issues from that.

Tim took my phone. He had already destroyed three or four phones in the past. I was in a corner; Tim had hit me a couple of times and spit on me. At that point I was trying to defuse the situation by asking him questions.

He kept saying, "I love you so much."

I said, "What makes you think that this is love? Please explain it to me."

I was trying to keep him talking, hoping that the police would get there soon. I wasn't sure if he was there to kill me or try to get me back.

The police got there and asked if I wanted to press charges. Tim started crying and swearing to God that he would leave me alone and act like he'd never known me. He said it would ruin his life if I pressed charges. I didn't want to ruin his life; I just wanted him to leave me alone, so I didn't press charges.

Three days later, he was calling again. He said he'd found a counselor and just wanted to be my friend.

I had moved from the house I rented to a townhouse that was closer to the city and I wasn't so isolated.

My ex-husband and I started dating and that lasted for about three months. I was heartbroken. Tim called about a month later, around Valentine's Day, and asked me out to lunch. We started dating again. He started back to church and things were going well. He gained my trust again.

One day we decided to go away for the weekend, just the two of us. I left the kids with a babysitter and off we went. About an hour into the trip, we were talking and laughing; things were great. I started picking with him about the fact that he had to match all his clothes and jewelry like a girl.

He flipped a switch. He started cussing and I said, "I don't want to do this, I want to go home."

He said, "No, don't even think about it. You're going whether you want to or not." He said, "Don't push me or you'll ruin the whole trip."

I then tried to smooth things over and act like nothing happened. We got to our destination, had dinner and started walking around town. I spotted a painting in a shop that I wanted to look at and I walked about five feet in front of him. He started saying that I had abandoned him, that I didn't need him and that I was acting like I didn't know him. I started trying to find an exit so I could get public transportation to get home. We were back out on the sidewalk and I spotted a police officer. I started walking fast and that gave away my plan to try and get away from him. He grabbed the back of my neck under my hair where no one could see what he was doing and turned me around. I got away from him and started screaming for help but no one would help me. The officer had apparently gone into a store and couldn't hear me.

Tim grabbed my wrist and bent it backwards and had me by the back of my neck, too. He dragged me into the hotel, which was close to where we were. There was no one at the desk. When we got to the room, he let me go. I started packing my things. He kept grabbing my stuff so I couldn't pack it. A marijuana joint fell out of the stuff and I got mad that he had drugs around me. I tried calling the front desk but he broke the phone. I tried leaving the room but he grabbed me and wouldn't let me go. I tried kicking the door, hoping that someone would hear me and call the front desk or the police.

I asked him why he always had to ruin everything.

He said, "I don't like your fucking attitude, you're the one that ruins everything." He started to slap me and I put my hand up to block him and he grabbed the top of my first three fingers and slowly bent them back until they broke. I was crying and screaming. I slept with an icepack all night.

Tim lay closest to the door but didn't sleep. Every time I looked at him, he was awake.

I played along like everything was okay the next day because I just wanted to get home without any more injuries. When we got back, the babysitter knew something was wrong so she stayed until he left.

Tim and I broke up and got back together several times. He broke down the door at the townhouse more than once.

One time I had decided to stay with a friend for a few days. We both had kids and they all got along really well. I had gone by the townhouse by myself to get some clothes and when I opened the door to leave, there he was. He had a knife in his hand. He got me by my hair and started dragging up the stairs. I was trying to fight him off. All the pictures of me and my kids got broken. They were on the wall going up the stairs. It was only by the grace of God that I got away from him that night.

I tried avoiding him all that I could. One day he saw me at a gas station, came up, grabbed my phone and crushed it, then got me by my hair and pulled out a clump of it. I was screaming as I ran into the store telling the cashier to call the police. Tim knew the police were coming so he left.

I realized that I needed to move far away from him. My ex-husband and I decided to work things out and I'm happy to say my life is good now.

In the year and a half to almost two years that Tim and I were together, we broke up probably a dozen times.

If I could say one thing to help someone that is in a abusive relationship, it would be to pay attention to the red flags. You can't change him and you can't fix him.

Our strength is shown in the things we stand for.
Our weakness is shown in the things we fall for.
— Vernon K. McLellan

May you have the hindsight to know where you have been, the foresight to know where you're going, and the insight to know when you've gone too far.
— Irish blessing

Chapter 4

You're Stronger Than You Think— Don't Give Up

WHEN THE ABUSE STARTS IN the relationship, you're in shock. Next you're embarrassed and ashamed. You try to justify what happened so you can understand it. The first time you tell someone what happened to you, it's hard to talk about it; but you soon realize the more you talk about it, and the more people you tell, you start to feel yourself getting stronger. Some people heal quicker than others. Take your time. Some people will not believe you. Continue to talk to those who believe you and will support you. If someone offers you their phone number to call any time of day or night, then take it. You have a life-or-death situation, and you'll need to be able to act fast and have someone there quickly.

When you finally realize that your abuser is not going to change, and you need to get out, then reach out. You might not realize it, but there are people who care about you. It might be family, friends, or both. Start by letting people you trust know what's going on. The more you talk about it, the stronger you'll get. It takes real inner strength to leave an abusive situation. It takes time to build that strength. The more you reach out, the faster that strength builds.

You might be in a situation where you don't have family or trusted friends close by, but there are still people you can go to and explain what you're up against. Find someone you can trust. It may be your boss or the lady at the register at the grocery store. Bond and find security in knowing that you don't have to do this alone. Churches, shelters, and other community places are sources you can check with for help. Co-workers might be somewhere you can start. Don't give up.

I know you probably feel like life isn't going to get any better and at least this life is predictable. Stop thinking like that. Life can be good. You're alive and you need to live. Get your eyes off the floor and realize that outside this abuse, you can live again. You can laugh and be yourself without judgment. You can learn to make decisions on your own. You can do this. I know you can. Talk about it, talk about it, talk about it. You will feel the life coming back into your body. Slowly but surely, it will come. A word of advice: you might not want to discuss your situation with your abuser's family right away. It might be harmful or fatal. It doesn't matter how close you are to them. Blood ties are thick. Be careful.

I know it might be hard to remember when you felt good about yourself. It might be hard to remember when you felt good about anything. Don't give up; you deserve better. You might not think so now, but give yourself a break and give yourself time. Keep looking up. There's a brighter tomorrow. There might be friends and even family members that turn their backs on you because

You're Stronger Than You Think—Don't Give Up

you've left and gone back multiple times before. They've given up on you, but you can't give up on yourself. Hold steady to the ones that are holding on to you because they want to help. You will probably be surprised at how many people want to help but just don't know how. Sometimes all you need is for someone to listen, not judge, not give advice, just listen to your story. All victims have one. Some are short stories and some are more like a series. Strength in numbers. Surround yourself with people whom you can draw strength from. I know you might be thinking, "I just can't do it. I don't have the energy. I'm drained—physically, mentally, emotionally, financially, spiritually, etc." You can do it.

Do it for yourself. If you can't do it for you, then do it for your kids, your family, your friends, anybody: just do it. Learn to trust again so you can be a survivor. Don't be a victim anymore. A good source of strength is a survivor of domestic violence. That person could be your lifeline to connect with. Relating stories to one another helps you realize that you're not alone. You are unfortunately part of a huge number of victims. In weaving yourself in and around strong people, you can make yourself a part of that blanket of protection. Protect what's left of your damaged mind and body. Let the healing begin. Let yourself feel the patching of emotions, the threads of hope weaving your shattered life back together. It will start to heal you from the inside out. Don't give up.

Take baby steps, then bigger steps, then jumps, and then leap for joy. You're on your way to happiness. It's not far. You'll probably hit a few dips in the road to recovery and freedom, but guess what? You're moving in the right direction. You're going somewhere. Set a goal and reach for it. Grab it. It's yours. Give yourself a pep talk and think positive. Start rebuilding what has been torn down. Put one foot in front of the other. Soon you'll be walking out that door: a door that will lead to peace and contentment, a door to freedom. Open it—it's waiting. Get up, don't stay in this mess. Get up and be free. Get up—you're stronger than you think. Get up and live.

Please realize that suicide and homicide are not options.

<u>Suicide</u> will get you out of the situation, but not alive. You hurt more than yourself. Family and friends are hurt also if you choose this way out. Please don't even think about suicide. There's always a way out and it will leave you alive.

<u>Homicide</u> will get you out of the abusive situation but it will land you right in the middle of trouble. There are times when you are in a situation of self-defense, but that doesn't mean they won't put you in jail.

You need to document any and all abuse anytime you can. Pictures and tape recordings of the abuse go a whole lot further in court than just writing it down. Writing it down could be your word against his. It would be really hard for him to prove his innocence when you have evidence there for the judge to hear and see.

Stephanie's Story

PETE AND I MET ONLINE. His lies and manipulation started from the beginning, but I didn't realize it until the very end. I thought he was the one. I had been married before and had two kids, but they were young adults. They saw right through Pete, but I was blinded by all the stuff he would say. I couldn't see the reality of it all.

One of his first big lies was when he said he wanted to take me to the beach for the weekend. He had a place down there and wanted to show it to me. I packed and was ready, but he never showed up. I finally heard from him on Monday and he said that the mother of his youngest son had died in a car accident. I went into "mom mode" and said that I would do whatever I needed to in order to help him and his son. Pete always had some excuse for why he couldn't see me every other weekend. He said he had to take his son to another state for the funeral. I said I would be glad to go and support him and his son. He said that he didn't want to get me involved because his ex-wife was a part of a biker gang, and that they were trying to take his son from him.

The next tale was that he, his son, and his mom were all in protective custody because his ex-wife's biker gang had attacked his mom in the Walmart parking lot. I soon found out that all of that was a lie, and that his ex-wife was alive and well. I confronted Pete about it, and he said he was just testing me to see if I'd stick around if something like that happened. It was one lie after another, but he was so good at it that most of the time I believed it.

Pete never hit me but he was so controlling, and I was so scared of him, that all he had to do was get mad and I would cower down like a whipped pup. He didn't want me around my friends or my family. It was a chore to go see my family out of state. He would always find a way to ruin every visit. He would show up at my job constantly, and he had me in tears on a regular basis. I felt so confused and messed up that I didn't know if I was coming or going. He had me second-guessing my own decisions all the time. He was so jealous and insecure that he would accuse me of cheating on him all the time. Pete lied so much that I didn't find out until later that I was his fourth wife. He would come and sit in the parking lot of my job, and he would call and call and call. If my boss and I were gone at the same time, Pete would accuse me of cheating. If I was just a few minutes late coming home from work, he would accuse me of having an affair with someone. I often wondered how he kept his own job because of how often he was always showing up at mine.

Pete didn't like anything or anyone that took attention away from him. My kids' dog had died, and Pete said that he would bury it for them. A day or so later my daughter wanted to go see the grave and we found out that Pete had thrown the dog in the woods and then just put some sticks over it. This was another devastating blow.

Stephanie's Story

Toward the end of our marriage, Pete suggested that I go to the beach place and take my kids with me for time with them. I knew something didn't sound right, but I missed being with my kids. I was ready to leave Pete anyway, and I was done with the lies and abuse. We went to the beach place, and I packed all my stuff that I'd left there. I was a nervous wreck, thinking he was going to show up any minute. He never showed up, and I found out it was because he had another woman sleeping in our bed while I was gone. I left the house very upset, and Pete called my daughter and told her that I was suicidal. My daughter called the police and then called me.

The police were at the house all day because Pete wouldn't let anyone come in but me; and he would only let people come to the porch to get one thing at a time. I asked Pete to please have his son go play at the neighbor's house, or have someone drive him around so he didn't have to see all of that, but Pete wouldn't do it. His son was seven years old and didn't need to be a part of any more drama, but it didn't matter to Pete.

I left twice in the three years we were together. I got a small portion of the money I had invested in the relationship and the home, but lost so much of myself. You never go back to being who you were before being in an abusive relationship; but you're stronger and wiser than before. If I could say anything to someone who is in an abusive relationship, it would be that you need to tell a friend what's going on. Tell a family member, ask for help. Don't be ashamed, and never feel like you're alone.

To conquer fear is the beginning of wisdom.
— Bertrand Russel

When you cannot make up your mind which of the two evenly balanced courses of action to take—choose the bolder one.
— W. J. Slim

Chapter 5

THIS IS NOT WHAT WE'RE MADE FOR — WHAT WE KNOW ABOUT HOW TO TREAT EACH OTHER

Here are Four Common Myths:

- *Myth #1: Some men can't help themselves. They can't control their anger.* If that's the case, then how are they able to control their anger on the job, on the highway or in a grocery store? Abusers need to be held accountable for their actions, no matter what excuses they use. If they're not, it only adds fuel to the fire that is already out of control.
- *Myth #2: Women who are abused only have themselves to blame.* Some people think that the victims drive their abusers over the edge. In some cases it may be true but that doesn't make it okay for the abuse. It is also said that the victims do it to get attention and sympathy from others, when in fact they keep it to themselves. Wife-battering is commonly known as the "silent crime" because they're

afraid to tell anyone due to the fact that the abuser may find out she's talking about it.

- *Myth #3: The Bible says that an abused woman must be willing to follow Christ's example of suffering and put up with her husband's anger and abuse.* The Bible does not promote anger or abuse. Ecclesiastes 7:9 says, "Be not hasty in your spirit to be angry; for anger rests in the bosoms of fools." Proverbs 14:7 says, "A quick-tempered man acts foolishly, and a man of wicked intentions is hated." Ephesians 4:31–32 says, "Let all bitterness, and wrath, and anger, and clamor, and evil speaking be put away from you, with all malice; And be ye kind to one another, even as God for Christ's sake hath forgiven you." A wife has a good reason to follow her husband if he loves, leads, and sacrifices as Jesus did for the church.
- *Myth #4: The Bible says a wife should submit to her husband in everything, including abuse.* The Bible does in fact say that a wife should be submissive to her husband, but it never says she has to tolerate abuse. Ephesians 5:24-25 says, "Therefore as the church is subject unto Christ, so let the wives be to their own husbands in everything. Husbands love your wives, even as Christ also loved the church, and gave himself for it." Ephesians 5:28 says, "So ought men to love their wives as their own bodies. He that loveth his wife loveth himself." Colossians 3:19 says, "Husbands, love your wives, and be not bitter against them." The kinder a man is to his wife, the more she would want to be submissive to him, but if a husband turns to abuse to control his wife and

This Is Not What We're Made For

child, then the wife has to do whatever she can to protect herself and her child.

For Heaven's Sake
Live to breath.
Live to walk without fear of being knocked down.
Live to run without being chased.
Live to laugh without being scared to be yourself.
Live to smile at a stranger without fear of a jealous rage.
Live to live.
Live to love yourself and those around you.
That's what God wants for us, to live.

No God, no peace. Know God, know peace.

The Cycle of Battering

1. Tension-Building
2. Explosion
3. Love

First: Tension-Building

- The victim senses the abuser's edginess.
- The victim usually denies the abuser's anger.
- The victim often feels the anger is deserved.
- The victim denies that the explosion phase will occur and believes the abuse can be controlled.
- The victim often withdraws in order to "not" set off the abuser.
- The abuser's jealousy and smothering increases.
- Tension continues to rise.
- At this stage, the victim is so stressed that he or she is almost at the point of being physically sick.
- Often the victim knows the explosion is going to happen so they provoke the abuser just to get it over with.

Second: Explosion

- Usually the abuser's initial goal is not to hurt the victim, but to teach the victim a lesson.
- The victim can usually describe the explosion stage in detail but the abuser can't.

- In this stage only, victims often feel it's okay to get angry and fight back.
- This is the shortest stage and generally lasts from a few hours to forty-eight hours.
- We don't know why the abuse finally stops (possibly exhaustion) but the abuser usually knows how long to prolong the abuse without killing the victim.
- Very often the victim will deny the seriousness of the injuries, to soothe the abuser and to assure that this stage is over.

Third: Love (also known as the honeymoon stage)

- This stage is welcomed by both.
- The abuser is sorry and tries to make up with flowers, candy, jewelry and all in excess.
- The abuser feels like the victim will leave.
- The abuser is charming and manipulative.
- The victim wants to believe the abuser will change.
- The abuser says the abuse is under control and the victim will not be hurt again.
- Often the abuser says he will fall apart without the victim.
- The abuser will often cry and say he needs help and is going to seek treatment but never does.
- This stage is usually longer than stage two, the explosive stage, but shorter than stage one, the tension-building stage.

Can You See the Signs

We are not meant to be punching bags for anyone. We are made to be a helper for our mate, not beneath them to be trampled on, not behind them to be led like a dog or a prisoner, but to walk beside our mate, hand in hand, to be cherished like a friend or the other half of one's self.

It's hard to have a good relationship if the person you're with is not your friend.

The physical connection only lasts so long; after that you need to be able to laugh, cry, and support each other through the rest of your lives.

Don't walk in front of me, for I may not follow. Don't walk behind me, for I may not lead. Just walk beside me, and be my friend.
— Author unknown

Christy's Story

Brian and I were childhood sweethearts. We started partying as a teens, drinking and doing drugs, and then I got pregnant. We got married, moved to a different state, and he started working out of town five days a week. I stayed home and took care of the baby and the house. When he came home on weekends, he would be angry as soon as he came through the door. He started calling me a slut, and accusing me of cheating on him while he was gone. After two years of constant verbal and mental abuse, I decided I'd been accused of running around enough. I decided to actually go out and have a fling as revenge, and so I did. I went out, met a guy and had a one-night stand. We never had a relationship.

Not long after that, my brother-in-law, Tim, his wife, Suzie, and their child moved in with us. My brother-in-law started working out of town with Brian. Suzie and I would sometimes get a babysitter and we'd go out drinking. I met a guy, Chris, I was physically attracted to and ended up leaving my husband for him. It was all about sex. He started being abusive before we ever got married, but I married him anyway. At this point in my life, I was emotionally dependent and emotionally weak. One day we were at the river and we had been canoeing with a friend of his. When we got out of the water, Chris shoved me down so hard the fall broke my collarbone. We had to call 911. He ended up taking care of me because I didn't know anyone else around that I knew well enough to ask for help. We were only married eight months. After I left, he would stalk me. He followed me everywhere. One day after I dropped my daughter off at school, I was leaving and I saw Chris in a parking lot yelling and honking the horn at me. He was motioning for me to come over to him. I was so mad that I not only went over there but I also T-boned his car. The law was called, but no charges were pressed. He finally left me alone. I gained confidence in myself and realized that I was emotionally strong and didn't need him.

I was single for eight years. I wanted revenge on men in general, so I used a few for everything I could get, then left them, but then I started going to church, got saved and wanted to live my life differently. I met Matt at church. He got saved and baptized. We were just friends for about a year and a half. I felt like God had sent this man to me so we got married. My child Sandy was now fifteen. We were married about two or three months, and Sandy and Matt were arguing. I was in the bathroom, and I said something that let Matt know that I was defending Sandy. He came in the bathroom and slapped me, kicked a hole in the wall, and stormed out. He didn't abuse me for a while after that. Sandy decided to move in with her biological dad because she didn't like the rules at our house. In the period of time Sandy was gone, Matt blacked my eye one time. There were several years after that when he didn't abuse me at all. This was my third marriage and I wanted it to work so

Christy's Story

badly. I had the preacher talk to Matt and things seemed to be okay. Early in our marriage, Matt had suffered with depression and was treated for it. Now he said that he was feeling depressed again, and I got worried. My mom and stepdad were coming down to see us and I wanted it to go smoothly. It did.

Soon Matt started talking about wanting to kill his ex-wife because of child support. It scared me so much that when he went to his dad's the next day I loaded up all the guns and took them to the sheriff's department. I took out papers to have him committed. Long story short, he was picked up, sent somewhere else, then released. The sheriff brought him home. After they left, he got extremely angry and was acting very unstable. He didn't touch me until the next day. He walked in the living room, grabbed me by the throat, and choked me until I couldn't breathe. When he finally let go, I grabbed the phone and called 911 when he wasn't looking. They came and took him away and said I needed to take a restraining order out on him because they saw the marks on my throat, so I did. I stayed in the house for a while; then Matt's sister called and said he really needed to come home. I decided to move out, but didn't take much.

It was about a month or so later that Matt checked himself into the hospital. He was diagnosed with bipolar disorder and was taken off the anti-depressant drugs and was put on the right meds. He agreed to go see a Christian counselor. He was back in church, but I wouldn't go around him except for counseling. I was still afraid of him. He got up in front of the church and told the congregation everything he'd done, and then he asked for forgiveness. He said he wanted to do whatever it took to get me back. We had been separated two and a half months then, and I moved back in.

For seven years, things were good. There was no abuse, but we had drifted apart. Matt quit going to church, but I kept going. I even tried going to different churches so he would go with me, but he'd go for a few weeks and then quit. I got closer to the Lord as Matt got further away. My stepdad had passed away, so I'd go up to my mom's at Thanksgiving and decorate her house for Christmas. Matt kept calling over and over. I finally told him that I was going to leave him as soon as I got home.

I left my mom's the next morning. Matt called me on my way home and asked if I was still going to leave him; I told him that I was. I found out later that he had called my mom and said the devil can make you do all kinds of things. When I got home, Matt was there, but he was supposed to be at work. He had left his job and there wasn't anyone covering his shift. I wasn't afraid because he hadn't given me any reason to be afraid for a really long time. I was in the kitchen getting ready to wrap a set of dishes that was a family heirloom, and Matt came in with a .380 pistol and said, "You're not coming back," and he started shooting. He shot both my legs and I fell to the floor. I was in shock. He wasn't rapidly shooting me. He'd shoot, then wait a minute, and then shoot again. Then he shot two more times. He left the room and I remember praying. Then Matt came back in the room with a 9mm pistol. He was standing about ten feet from me; I remember looking up at the phone, but the phone wasn't on the receiver. Matt pointed the pistol at me, and at that point I had accepted the fact that I was going to die. I started wondering what it would feel like to be shot in the head. Would I die quickly? Would everything just go black? I curled up in a ball as best I could with my injuries, and I got behind the wooden counter knowing that if he shot, it wouldn't protect me. I waited and waited, then I peeked out and saw him messing with the gun. When he saw me, he pointed the gun at me again. I got back behind the counter, and waited for the shot. I peeked out again, and he was messing with the gun again. Then pointed it at me. I kept waiting for the shot and it didn't come. I looked again and he was still messing with the gun, so I said, "Matt, are you going to kill me," and he said, "Yeeaah." He said, "You're not going to stay now."

That clued me in on what to say and I'm sure the Holy Spirit did too. I said, "Granted, we have a lot to work through, but I'm not dead yet and you haven't been charged with murder."

He said, "There ain't no way you'd stay now."

I asked him, "Have I ever left you permanently?"

He told me that I was lying. I told him that if I was going to leave him permanently, I wouldn't have agreed to go to the doctor with him next month. I told him to think about my mother and his daughter. Then I prayed, "Lord Jesus be with my husband." Matt said he was going to have to do something because I was losing a lot of blood. I told him that I was getting lightheaded, that I probably wasn't going to be on earth much longer. He decided to call 911, but had to hook the phone back up on the wall because he had unhooked it while planning out what he was going to do earlier. I told him that he was going to have to go outside after he called 911 because they wouldn't come in until things were secure. He gave the operator his name, told them what he'd done, and told them he'd be in the front yard when they got there. When he hung up, he called one of his coworkers, told him what he'd done, and told him that he needed him to go to work to cover his shift. The coworker couldn't believe what Matt was saying, so Matt calmly repeated it again. He hung up the phone and then got his guns together. I had a fear that he was going to turn around and finish me off, so I said, "See you soon, I love you," hoping he'd just keep going. It wasn't long before I heard sirens, and then I heard someone tell Matt to get on the ground. Soon after that, I heard someone come inside.

On the way to the hospital I blacked out. I had several emergency surgeries. I had internal bleeding, my leg was broken, and I had fluid in my stomach. I had to have my left ovary and my left fallopian tube removed and my uterus repaired. I had to have my small intestines repaired and a section of my large intestines removed. I had to wear a colostomy bag for a while. Matt was sentenced to nine to thirteen years in prison.

We were married for thirteen years. If there was one thing I could say to someone who is involved in an abusive relationship, it would be that without divine intervention, your abuser is not going to change. He has to be willing.

The only courage that matters is the kind that gets you from one minute to the next.
— Mignon McLaughlin

What soap is to the body, tears are to the soul.
— Jewish proverb

If you can learn from hard knocks, you can also learn from soft touches.
— Carolyn Kenmore

Chapter 6

Recovery Takes Time and Help

So you've finally escaped your abusive relationship. Please realize that just because you're out of that relationship doesn't mean you're not still a victim. Recovery takes time, sometimes a long time. Don't suppress your feelings, and don't hide what you've been through. Talk about it. Find someone who will listen to everything you're saying, whether it's a friend, relative, church member, or someone at a battered women's shelter. It's very therapeutic to express in detail the pain and suffering you endured. It also releases it from you, which helps you gain confidence and peace in yourself. Purge your system. It's amazing how much better you will feel. Be prepared for the people that won't want to hear what you have to say. There will be some that say, "You're out of it. Get over it." They don't understand that it's not that easy. People don't usually mean to be cruel when they say that, but so many people don't have a clue as to what you survived. Physical abuse heals sometimes with no scars.

Emotional scars can leave such a massive wound that you don't think you can ever heal, but give yourself time. Cry, get mad, have a pity party or ten, but let yourself grieve. Tell someone, write it down. If you don't write well, put it on a tape recorder. Purge yourself of all that garbage that has eaten at you for so long. Trust me, it helps. Sometimes family and close friends don't want to know all the details, they're just glad you're safe; but telling the details is one of the things that helps you heal. Find someone who will listen. Try to write down or at least be aware of things, places, or people that trigger bad memories. Take your time, but realize that being a victim is like being a prisoner: you don't just get away from the prison and everything is lovely. There's hurt and pain that only time and the help of others can heal.

Try to turn the heartache to laughter. Practice laughing because you're free and you can laugh all you want. Don't let your suffering consume you. Sometimes staying in that mode of helplessness is easier than trying to change your outlook on life. Learning to look on the bright side of things is a mindset that should be practiced daily. Smile, look people in the eye. You can do it. It feels great. Talk to the man or woman at the checkout, be alive. Tell someone you're having a great day. You have a voice: let it be heard.

This section of this chapter is for family and friends of the victim.
Here are a few things that are helpful in dealing with the victim, Do's and Don'ts that can help.

Don't Say:

- "I don't want to get involved, it's none of my business." It is your business to help and protect the person you care

Recovery Takes Time and Help

about. "Did you do or say something to make him mad?" No matter what was said or done, there's no excuse for abuse.

- "Well, he seems like such a nice person to me." Abusers can be very good at playing different roles. A lot of times other people don't see what the abuser is doing to the victim. It is done in secret and behind closed doors.
- "It can't be that bad." Until someone has experienced abuse themselves, it's not right or fair to assume that what that victim has been or is going through is not that bad. Walk a mile in their shoes, then see what you have to say.
- "He's a jerk, how could you care about someone who does that to you?" Victims don't fall in love with someone because they're being abused by that person. The abuser was probably charming, and pretended to have great qualities. The abuser's true colors usually show after the victim has fallen for him. The victim then wants to believe that the abuser will change back to her prince charming. Love is blind and hopeful. There have been times when abusers have changed. They just have to want to change.
- "Why didn't / don't you just leave?" That's easier said than done. A lot of times the victim has been abused so much that she doesn't have the strength to leave. It seems easier to just stay and put up with it. Most of the time, the victim has no self-esteem left and no willpower to change her circumstances.
- "You're the one that chose him—deal with it." Yes, she chose him, but that doesn't mean that she chose to be beaten.

When two people meet and then fall in love, she has the hope of loving and being loved. She doesn't sit around and think, "Oh boy, maybe I'll get abused."

- "Divorce is a sin." Nowhere in the Bible does it state that a woman should put up with abuse. Divorce is never a good thing but when you say till death do you part, it doesn't mean until he beats her to death.
- "If you won't help yourself, why should I help you?" So many times victims want to get help, they want to leave, they want a better life, but they can't do it by themselves. If you are a friend or family member, you need to make sure that victim knows you're there and ready to help carry her.
- Don't question the abuser; you could be setting your friend or loved one up for another beating or worse—to be killed.

Do Say:

- "I'm worried about you. Would you like to talk about it?"
- "No one deserves to be treated like that. What can I do to help?"
- "There's no excuse for abuse: physical, emotional, financial, etc. None of it is okay. It's not uncommon for an abuser to act one way in front of people and another way in front of the person being abused. It's hard when the one you love treats you badly.
- "I know you love him, you just want him to stop hurting you."
- "Sometimes the only way to stop the abuse is to get away from the abuser. Have you thought about that?'

Recovery Takes Time and Help

- "He needs help. He can't stop on his own. If he doesn't see what he's doing is wrong, he's not going to change."
- "We don't always see the signs of abuse when we're falling in love, and then we don't want to believe that it's really happening until the damage is done."

Teresa's Story

I HAD BEEN SINGLE FOR a number of years. I worked lots of hours, so I really didn't know how to meet people. I decided to get on a dating website and that's how I met James. We talked several times on the phone before meeting face to face. I was forty years old at the time. At first James seemed perfect, but looking back, there were a lot of red flags that I was too blind to see then. He liked sneaking in my apartment and scaring me. He thought that was funny. To begin with James would go to church with me because he knew that meant a lot to me, but then he started picking fights on the way to church and I'd be too upset to go in and he'd say, "Why don't we just go home?" James would want to make up when we got home.

We only dated a few months. It was a whirlwind romance and then we got married. He seemed to read me well and knew how to do or say what I needed done or said. He lead me to believe that he'd only been married one time, was divorced, and had two kids. Looking back now, there were so many lies that it's amazing that he pulled it off. He said he had full custody of his kids, the youngest being one and a half years old.

Teresa's Story

James said he worried that when his son went to see his biological mom that he would be hurt or abducted because she was part of a biker gang. He also said he had a degree in engineering, was a third-degree black belt, and was in competitions on ESPN. He said he was a drummer and a musician. He said the house he moved us into was purchased after his divorce, and that his ex-wife had never lived in it. These were all lies. I also found out that he had a third child when the child showed up at the door one day after we were married. To make matters worse, when I met his family, no one said anything, so I thought what he said was true. I learned that they lied too.

We hadn't been married long when he got furious with me when I asked about how to work the programmable thermostat. I thought to myself, "Oh my gosh, who are you and who did I marry?" I thought he was going to hit me but he didn't. He didn't break stuff, but he'd throw dinner sometimes for various reasons, never any that made any sense. He said that he loved animals, but when I moved in he wanted me to get rid of my dog. Every time I wanted to get away from him, I would take my dog and go drive around. One time I couldn't find my dog so I left, but James called and told me to come get my dog or he was going to kill him. I could hear my dog yelping in the background. I went back.

One day I came home and my dog was gutted and lying in the garage but he was still alive. I wrapped him in a sheet and took him to the vet. James denied that he'd done anything and that he must have gotten run over by a car. We lived on a cul-de-sac so that story didn't make sense. I couldn't prove it but I believe James did it. My dog had to be put to sleep. The only thing James said was, "I didn't realize how attached you were to that dog."

He convinced me that we needed to put all our money together, even the retirement accounts. He had control of all the finances. I always tried to keep peace so he wouldn't get angry, but it didn't matter what I did. He always found something to get angry about. He would control me by embarrassing me because he knew I couldn't take being embarrassed. He even accused me of sleeping with my cousins.

James would keep me up all night fighting. He used fear to intimidate me. He wouldn't let me out of the bathroom, or any room. He acted like a bully. He would hide my stuff and I never got it back. He would jerk the covers off of me in the middle of the night, get inches from my face and start screaming at me. He would accuse me of sleeping with someone I spoke to that day or scream at me about a past relationship I had before I knew him.

I didn't get more than two hours of sleep at a time. Then in the morning, he'd make a chore list like I was a kid. He harassed me all day long while I was at work. I could hardly function because I was so sleep deprived. He would either call me every few minutes or show up at my job if I didn't answer his calls right away. He wanted me to quit my job and stay home, but he wanted me to make money too. He would put me down, saying that I wasn't being a good wife or a good stepmom.

He convinced me to lie at my job so I'd get fired and get unemployment. I received a check and then I called to stop them because I didn't think it was right. James was furious. I got temporary jobs, and he would sit in the parking lot while I worked.

Teresa's Story

When his youngest child came for visitation, things were a lot better. I poured my love on him. He was what kept me going. He was only two. I love him today as much as if I'd given birth to him.

James would go back to being a bully when we were alone. I feel like he had sexual issues. Sometimes when I took a shower he would pull the shower curtain back and just stare, not saying a word. It was creepy. He didn't care how sick I was or what was wrong with me, he demanded sex. I now know what it feels like to be raped. He would have sex with me and just smile.

James would get so out of control that I would just leave. He would take my car keys and my phone so I'd just start walking. He would come pick me up and then make fun of me because he knew I had no family or friends close by to rescue me. He never did drugs or drank. He just loved being a bully. He was evil and loved the reactions he got from me. I felt like I was losing my mind towards the end, so I started fighting back.

He backed off sometimes. I could tell when he would start to lose control because he would smell different and his face would change. I was very scared at these times more than others. I became so disconnected. I knew I needed to get out but wasn't sure how. I knew I would be homeless but I needed to leave.

The last day I was there, he said he was going to work late but came home early, got mad because I had already eaten, and threw his food across the room. I kept thinking that if I had a gun I'd shoot him and stop that noise coming out of his mouth. I told him if he didn't leave that I'd kill him, so he packed a bag and left. I threw some clothes in a trash bag and left before he came back. I dumped the change jar in a bag too. I stayed in a motel one night, the Walmart parking lot one night, and at a friend's house some. I never went back. I never got all my stuff back either, but I feel like he would have killed me if I had stayed.

I left six times altogether. We were together a total of two years. If I could say something to someone who is going through this, it would be: you're not alone, and there are people who understand and want to help. You'll never be the same.

If you're going through hell, keep going.
— Winston Churchill

In the end, it's not the years in your life that count.
It's the life in your years.
— Author Unknown

Some of us think holding on makes us strong,
but sometimes it is letting go.
— Hermann Hesse

Chapter 7

WHAT ABOUT THE CHILDREN? HOW DOES IT AFFECT THEM?

CHILDREN ARE AFFECTED EVEN WHEN they're not being abused themselves.

- They may be scared.
- They can feel guilty, thinking it's their fault.
- They might start feeling bad about themselves and feel insecure.
- They may lose love and respect for their parents.
- They can be angry at the abuser for being mean to the other parent.
- They may feel anger toward the victim for not leaving the abusive situation and for not protecting them from being exposed to it.
- They might say they were cheated out of a "normal family life."
- They may feel neglected, powerless, and alone.

- They may feel confused and not sure whose side to be on, or if they have to choose.
- They might feel like they can't trust anyone.
- They may think that they could get injured or killed.
- They may want to seek revenge.
- They might become withdrawn and shy.
- They might act older than their age, in order to attempt to take care of and protect their mother.
- They may decide to use drugs and alcohol to deal with their feelings.
- They might grow up and have no respect or trust for the opposite sex.
- They might grow up to be abusive, or end up being abused themselves as an adult.
- They might not even have their own basic needs met.
- They could have problems in school and decide that running away is the answer.

A lot of times the victim doesn't realize that the children are being affected by the presence of domestic violence. The victim will try to cover up the bruises and to make excuses for the abuser. The victim is trying to survive, not seeing that her children are having their world torn apart too. Girls tend to marry men like their fathers without realizing it. If their father was abusive, it is likely that they will marry an abuser.

Both parents need to realize what domestic violence does to the children. Children should be taught what to do when the abuse starts, where to go, and who to call. Victims should not belittle

What About the Children? How Does it Affect Them?

their abuser to the kids. For one thing, the abuser could be the children's father. Kids can get confused and take sides. No child should have to choose one or the other. Don't unload or give details about the abuse to the children. They're having a tough enough time trying to deal with it. A lot of times when the victim gets out of the situation, or the abuse stops, there isn't time spent with the children to find out their feelings.

It's always a good idea to seek counseling for your children. The trauma that they have experienced is very real. They need a neutral person who won't take sides. A counselor who is trained to deal with children who has been a victim or witnessed domestic violence would be the best for the children to see. Kids will say things sometimes just because they know it's what one parent wants to hear. Then they will tell the other parent what he or she wants to hear. They're just protecting themselves.

Protect the children. Protect their minds and their bodies. What they experience as a child can have a lifetime impact on them. Let them know that there's no excuse for abuse. Let them know that no matter what happens they are loved. Showing you love your child through thick and thin could be one of the best learning tools they'll ever see.

My life is my message.
— Mahatma Gandhi

Every day brings new choices.
— Martha Beck

Train up a child in the way he should go:
and when he is old he will not depart from it.
— Proverbs 22:6

Rights of a Battered Woman

- She has the right to not be abused.
- She has the right to be angry over past beatings.
- She has the right to choose to change the situation she's in.
- She has the right to freedom from fear of abuse.
- She has the right to request, and expect, assistance from the police and or social agencies.
- She has the right to share her feelings, and not be isolated from others.
- She has the right to want a better role model for her children.
- She has the right to be treated like an adult.
- She has the right to leave a battering environment.
- She has the right to privacy.
- She has the right to express her own feelings and thoughts.
- She has the right to convey her thoughts, and know that information will remain confidential.
- She has the right to develop her own talents and abilities.
- She has the right to legally prosecute the abusing partner or spouse.
- She has the right to not be perfect.
- She has the right to control her own finances.
- She has the right to have control over all aspects of her life.
- She has the right to be the woman she wants to be.

Suzanne's Story

I MET MY ABUSER THROUGH a friend in high school. It was Pete's brother. Pete told me not to date him, but sparks were there as soon as we met, so I wasn't listening to his advice. Gary was seven years older than I. I was eighteen at the time. We lived together for about four years. He sent me flowers and was very romantic. We were engaged for a year. Everyone thought he was a dream; I thought he was a dream. We had only been married for one week the first time Gary slapped me. We had a dinner party at our house a week after our honeymoon. When I closed the door after the last person left, I turned around and he smacked me. I was shocked; I wasn't sure what just happened. He was yelling a list of things I had done wrong. He said I flirted with his friends, there were spots on the glasses, I didn't clear the dishes quick enough, and he went on and on about how I embarrassed him.

In this time period, there wasn't a lot of knowledge about abuse. Women didn't leave, and the police would not take your side. I called 911 one time. They talked to him out on the front porch for a few minutes and then they started laughing. They came in and started in on me like I was the one who had done something wrong. I was the one bleeding. They wanted to know if I'd been taking any drugs, and what I had done to cause Gary to get upset. He was the one that smelled like alcohol. I remember screaming at the police, "I'm the one bleeding and you're questioning me, not him!"

Gary drank a lot, and sometimes smoked pot too. I found out that his father was very verbally abusive to his mom, but never physically. I remember his dad abusing his mom at our engagement party. Gary acted embarrassed, but then ended up acting ten times worse. After the first time I went to the hospital, his mom came up to see me and wanted to know what I had done to aggravate her son to cause him to act like that. She said I needed help and she would be happy to go with me. I had two children with Gary. My daughter said she used to have nightmares after she'd hear the screaming and crying. She is an adult now and is in an abusive relationship. It's mentally abusive so far. My son ended up being a controller. In his relationships, he can do what he wants but the girlfriend can't do anything. If a girl ever says anything about my son being abusive, I will not defend my son. I will not condone abuse.

I didn't think Gary would ever try to kill me; it seemed like he always knew when to quit. One time he broke my ring finger. He ripped all the phones out of the wall and told me that we weren't going anywhere until we had our stories straight. He kept screaming at me until I repeated everything he wanted me to say. When we got to the hospital, the nurses thought he was just being protective, but the doctor saw through it. When the X-rays came back, the doctor asked Gary to leave the room. Gary glared at me so I'd say I wanted him to stay, but I didn't. The doctor told me that he had to report the abuse or he'd be in trouble. I kept trying to stick to the lie but the doctor wasn't buying it. I was embarrassed because I worked at that hospital. When I went back to work, the nurses said they wished they had someone that cared for them like Gary cared for me. I wanted to puke.

I left the first time and my friends couldn't believe I would leave because I got a new car every three months. Gary owned a car lot, so it wasn't hard for him to bring a car home. He would use them as guilt gifts but would take them away every time he got mad. I never went to my high school reunions because my friends never understood why I would leave him when he gave me so much. I got lots of jewelry for guilt gifts too. I tried to explain how mean he was but they'd just say, "Husbands and wives fight. It's normal." I started doubting my own sanity. I was raised in an abusive home; I guess that's why Gary would hurt me so badly, because I would fight back.

One of the times that Gary put me in the hospital, my dad came there with a gun to threaten him. I was sitting there on pain pills wondering if they were fighting over who had the right to abuse me. I felt so bad because for years I had gotten mad at my mom for putting up with my dad's abuse, and then I was doing the same thing. It got to the point where I didn't tell anyone anything anymore. I just covered up the bruises, marks and knots on my head and body. My mom came to me and said she knew what was going on. "There's no way you're that clumsy, and you're wearing long sleeves in the summer." She kept begging me to please get away from Gary before the police came and told them that I was dead.

I left. I got an apartment. At first he was still being mean, but then he started acting like he had when we first met. He was very kind and sweet, and told me that he needed help. He said he didn't

Suzanne's Story

want to be without me and the kids. He said he was worried about me, and that he was worried that someone would take advantage of me. I thought I'd finally gotten through to him, so I moved back home. In less than a week, the abuse started again. It was punishment for leaving. He told me that when he wanted me gone, he'd tell me. "You don't leave me, I'll tell you when to leave." I thought, "Oh no, I'm my mom. I'm doing the same thing my mom did."

I used to tell him that I was going to leave, but then I regretted that because of the abuse that always followed. I started planning. I kept remembering the time he came into the bathroom while I was cleaning up after he had beat me. I looked up and asked, "Why did you marry me?"

He said, "Because other guys couldn't believe I had a young wife that my brother was interested in too; and being the big brother, I know what's best."

That statement helped me realize that he never loved me, and that it was just a plan he had. He had been married before, and he cheated on her, but I don't know if he abused her. He kept saying that no one would want me because I had kids, and because I've been married before. At that time people didn't divorce. There were times I thought about killing him. I thought about the movie *The Burning Bed*. I wondered if I could go through with it, and if so if I could deal with having to pay for it. I would think about my kids, and I knew I couldn't do it. I remember when I left Gary. Both my grandmas were very embarrassed at their churches because of me. I was with him for five years. My oldest was four and the baby was just a few months old.

Can You See the Signs

Because of all the abuse, I have neck and back issues. I went to the chiropractor and he thought I'd been in multiple car accidents. I had to tell him my story.

If there's one thing I could say to someone else, it would be, "It's not your fault." They will try to make you feel like you have to fix it, but it's not up to you. It's their issues that they need help with. They will take it out on you but don't let them. No one has ever done anything in her lifetime to deserve being abused. You're the only one who can change the situation for yourself. You have to get help, so you can leave and not let him talk you into coming back. You've got to care about yourself and your children.

You may encounter many defeats, but you must not be defeated.
— *Maya Angelou*

Sometimes it's the smallest decisions that can change your life forever.
— Keri Russell

Every exit is an entry somewhere else.
— Tom Stoppard

Chapter 8

Where to Go for Help— Your Legal Rights

You can call the police or sheriff for immediate help. You have the right to remain silent, but if you do then you won't get help and the nightmare you've been through will continue to haunt you. Everything you say can and will be used to protect you from your abuser. You have the right to get a restraining order without an attorney. It is a legal way to help keep your abuser away from you. You have the right to file criminal charges against your abuser. You have the right to discuss your situation with any one you choose. Don't keep domestic violence a secret. You have the right to see a doctor for medical treatment, and to talk to a lawyer and get legal advice.

A Protective Order

The Protective Order is a good idea to have if you feel like you and your children are in danger. It is good documentation to show you have a problem with your abuser. The order is not a guarantee that your abuser will choose to leave you alone, but it's good to have so that in the event that he does come after you, it is on record that he's supposed to leave you alone.

A Protective Order may do more than just protect you and your children. It may also:

- Order him not to threaten, abuse, or harass you, your children, or your family on the phone (home or cell), computer, or in person
- Give you possession of the residence and all personal property located in the residence except for his personal clothing, toiletries, and tools of trade
- Give you possession and use of the car
- Order him to stay away from your home, workplace, your or your children's school, daycare, and any place you are seeking shelter
- Give you temporary custody of the minor children
- Keep him from owning or buying a firearm for the period of the order, and suspend a concealed handgun permit if he has one
- Have the sheriff or police department remove him from the home and help you return to the home safely
- Order the abuser to attend and complete an Abuser Treatment Program

You can charge your abuser with a crime, such as Assault on a Female or Communicating Threats. You will need to go to the magistrate's office for that.

Where to Go for Help—Your Legal Rights

Services Available in Many Areas (Check Your Area for Availability):

- Alcoholics Anonymous (AA): for people with alcohol abuse problems
- Al-Anon: for people involved with others that have alcohol problems
- Family Services Shelter: for temporary shelter of abused women and their children, including individual and family counseling and a 24-hour crisis line
- Family Services: for Time-Out counseling for men, women, children, and couples; the goal of this program is to stop the mental and physical abuse
- Department of Social Services: for a large range of services for families, including the investigation of suspected child abuse and neglect
- Narcotics Anonymous (NA): for people with drug abuse problems
- Nar-Anon: for those who are involved with someone who has drug problems
- SCAN: for parents with a history of child abuse or who are at risk of abuse; has 24-hour crisis line

Numbers You Might Need:

- City and County Emergency
- Police Department / Domestic Violence Division
- Clerk of Court's Office
- Magistrate's Office
- Legal Aid
- Lawyer Referral Services

Kelly's Story

Brad and I dated for one year before we got married. I knew within a few months of dating Brad that he had anger issues but he never got angry towards me. My father died a little while after we were married.

Brad had two kids and I had one son, Tommy. Only one of his children lived with us, and the other one came on weekends. Brad was controlling, but not enough to raise a red flag. I got up every day at 5:00 a.m. to fix his breakfast and to pack his lunch. One day I was sick and didn't get up, so when Brad came home he was very angry because he hadn't eaten all day. I asked him why he didn't stop and get something to eat. He got mad and said, "Don't ever do anything for me again." I said "okay" in a calm voice. He got angry and turned the coffee table over. He threw the phone across the room. I was in shock, and I started crying because he had never acted like that before. I turned the table back over and then went to pick up the phone. He said, "I got it." I said, "That's okay, I got it." Brad grabbed me by the arms and squeezed them really hard. I told him that he was hurting me. Even though he was holding my arms, I managed to hit him in the back with the phone. Within seconds,

Kelly's Story

he was on top of me on the couch, choking me until I blacked out. This was the beginning of a long road of abuse.

I wore turtlenecks and long-sleeved shirts to hide the bruises. The marks on my neck went away after about three days, but the ones on my arms took about three weeks. One day I was at the store and I had forgotten to wear long sleeves. I saw two of my friends, and one commented about the matching bruises. I lied as usual and went on my way. I was going to leave Brad, but he got on the floor, and cried, and begged me not to leave. He said he had never been abusive before and would never be abusive again. In the course of fifteen months, it happened nine more times. He would choke me or throw me across the room. One time I climbed out the window to get away from him. He'd always cry, and I'd give in. I left four times before I left for good. The third time I left, I was gone for six months. Brad started taking medication and went for counseling while I was gone. I thought he was a changed man, so I went back to him.

In about three weeks, it started again. I was on the phone one evening when he came home from work. I always tried to have supper ready and the house cleaned before he got home. The kids knew how he was, so they always made sure their rooms were clean so he wouldn't get mad at them. Brad went by me and I smiled at him. He went into the bathroom, and when he came out he made a smart remark about the fact that I had bought another T-shirt, even though I was working and bought them with my own money. I actually contributed more money to the bills than he did. I knew he was angry, so I got off the phone and went to the bedroom. Brad came in and told me to leave. I hollered for Tommy, my son, to pack a bag, and told him that we were leaving. I started packing a bag, but when I went to the bathroom to get my toothbrush, Brad wouldn't let me out of the bathroom. He knocked me backwards into the bathtub. When I got up, he jerked me to the floor by my hair and I started screaming. I screamed for Tommy to call 911. When I got up, Brad hit me with his open hand. In times past, he'd usually push me, choke me, or throw me. This was the first time he'd actually hit me. Then he hit me on the side of my head. It made me so dizzy that I could hardly think clearly or figure out what had just happened. He turned to walk away, and I punched him in the back of the head. Then he turned around. Mind you, he is a big man: 6'3", weighing about 250, whereas I weighed 130. I don't know what I was thinking. He put me in a headlock and was choking me. My feet weren't even touching the floor. I couldn't scream: I was just trying to breathe. I guess because everything got quiet, his son walked in and saw what was happening and said, "Daddy, let her go." And so he let me go.

At that point, 911 had called back and was asking my son several questions. He told them that his stepdad was choking his mom. They hung up and then called back again. This time Brad answered the phone and said that everything was fine. The dispatcher said they were going to send a sheriff to our home anyway. Brad told them to do whatever the fuck they wanted, but he calmed down after he got off the phone because he knew the police were on the way.

The police said for us to wait in the car. We waited for an hour. I ended up calling them three times. We sat there for an hour and a half, and they still hadn't come out. I called them back and told them that I wasn't going to wait any longer. I told the police I'd

Kelly's Story

meet them at the end of the road. When they finally came, they said they had to wait for backup. I told them my story, but they told me that because I didn't have a big gash that was bleeding, they couldn't arrest him. They said I'd have to go downtown and fill out papers to get a restraining order. It was midnight and I had to go to a friend's house with my son.

The next morning, I called to see if the police had picked Brad up yet, and they couldn't find the paperwork I filled out. An officer finally found the paperwork under some other paperwork on someone else's desk. The police went and arrested him about three hours later. They told me that I could go and get my stuff. I asked if I could have someone go with me, and they did.

We got back to the house and in just a few minutes, Brad and his stepdad pulled up. His stepdad had bailed him out of jail. The sheriff said I could only take the things that Brad said I could have. I had some money put up, but he found it. I got a few of my clothes, my son got all of his stuff, and we left. Brad begged me for a year to come back. He kept asking if I'd do things with him even though we weren't back as a couple. It seemed like the nicer I was, the more he demanded. It was like I was feeding this monster. He would get mad over the littlest things.

When we went out to eat, I had to either look at my plate or at him. If people spoke to me, I had to explain everything about who they were and how I knew them. Brad said he had never abused anyone before, but I found out that he had abused his ex-wives. He had been married three times, and had also abused girlfriends. He told me that he had never loved anyone like he loved me. I told him that I didn't understand. If he loved me so much, how could he abuse me? I didn't tell people what he had done because I was too embarrassed. I did subpoena his ex-wives when we went to court, but they didn't show up because they were afraid of him and two of them had kids with him. The court awarded my restraining order for a year, and charged him with assault on a female, but they didn't charge him with the choking, which would have been a felony. They said they couldn't see the marks on my neck. Brad lied in court, but they saw through it. I was with him a total of three years.

My preacher at the time kept telling me that I needed to stay with Brad even though the preacher knew about the abuse. I was thirty-three years old and had been married three times. I just wanted it to work. When Brad treated me well, things were great. I needed that because of the loss of my father, but the good didn't outweigh the bad.

My advice to anyone who is in an abusive relationship is, it won't stop. It's a cycle that gets worse and worse. I believe that if I had stayed with him, I'd be dead by now.

When we are no longer able to change a situation, we are challenged to change ourselves.
— Viktor E. Frankl

When something is important enough, you do it even if the odds are not in your favor.
— Elon Musk

What you do today can improve all your tomorrows.
— Ralph Marston

Chapter 9

Practice Personal Safety

Practicing personal safety is very important even after you're out of the situation.

Remember: he might not be done yet.

When You Are at Home:

- Always keep your exterior doors locked even when you're at home. Make it a habit and it will become a habit that will protect you.
- Have deadbolts installed two feet above your door locks. It has been proven that having the locks apart like that actually give the door more stability, which makes it harder to kick in.
- Keep windows closed and locked on the bottom level if at all possible. Windows can be an easy entrance. If any are broken, get them fixed as soon as possible.
- Always keep shrubbery trimmed under windows. Bushes

are a good hiding place for people up to no good.
- Install motion detector lights near exterior doors. Never open a door because you hear a noise. Be cautious. Be safe.
- If you see a suspicious person in your neighborhood, especially near your home, call the police. Better to be safe than sorry.
- Form a Neighborhood Watch program in your area.

Be Safe In & Out of Your Vehicle:

- Try to keep your vehicle in good running condition by performing regular maintenance.
- Try to make sure you always have enough gas. Don't chance running out.
- Know how to change a flat tire. Always keep a spare tire.
- At all times in your car, keep jumper cables, a flashlight, a few tools, an umbrella, and a blanket for bad weather.
- Make sure you keep your vehicle locked when you're in it and when you're not. Your abuser could be stalking you and get in your car when you're not around.
- Keep windows up as much as possible.
- Pay attention when you're driving. Try not to get distracted by the kids, the radio, or the phone. Watch vehicles around you. Be careful you're not being followed.
- Don't go out at night by yourself, if at all possible.
- Whether in daylight or dark, if someone tries to get you to stop or pull over while you're driving, go to the nearest

well-lit area or business where there are people around. If you're near a police station, go there.
- Avoid dead-end streets.

Protect Yourself:

- When you go somewhere, choose a parking spot that is open and offers the safest walking distance to where you're going.
- When returning to your vehicle, always have your keys out and ready.
- Carry a whistle or pepper spray.
- Be prepared to scream at the top of your lungs if your abuser shows up where he's not welcome.
- Pay attention to your surroundings.
- Walk with boldness and purpose.
- Learn how to shoot a gun.
- Take a self-defense course.
- Get in good shape physically, mentally, and spiritually.
- Surround yourself with happy people.
- Evil comes in all shapes, sizes, and colors. Just because the man walking up to you isn't your abuser doesn't mean he's safe. He could have hired someone to do you harm.
- Learn to love yourself. If you don't love yourself, you won't want to defend yourself.

Karen's Story

I met Bill at a state park where I was hanging out with my friends. He was with his friends. I was seventeen years old. We started dating, dated for a year, then lived together for a year. We got married, and then two weeks after we said "I do," the abuse started. I guess I was so shocked that I didn't know what to do. He made me feel like it was my fault.

I worked, and he worked when he felt like it. He had total control of the money. He did drugs, drank, and had affairs with other women. He didn't even care that I knew. He started driving a truck, but he called me constantly. I had to be at work or at home at all times. I did go to the grocery store, but I knew that if I didn't hurry, I'd be in trouble. He would call several times during the night just to make sure I was there. We had three kids and, unfortunately, they witnessed way too much. One time Bill broke my sternum, and another time he choked me until I passed out and wet myself. I had been beaten for so long that I didn't have the strength to leave.

A little while after my youngest son was born, I started smoking pot and doing cocaine. Then I started doing crack, and meth. I did it for six years, then I quit everything. I was so mad at myself for ever doing that to begin with, I never did it again. I knew I had to be there for my kids. Getting beaten up was a part of my life.

Day after day, year after year—time just keeps passing by and you don't even realize it's been twenty-one years. I had finally had enough.

The last time Bill beat me up, I got up off the floor and told him that if he was going to kill me, then he should kill me now because I was going to call the cops, and he was going to jail. That's what happened, and I took out a restraining order that day. All three of my kids now have issues because of the violence they witnessed.

A little while after I left, my nightmare came back. My teenage daughter was walking down the road, when her dad, my ex-husband Bill, pulled up and said he would take her to her boyfriend's house. He had convinced her that I wouldn't let her see her boyfriend. He kidnapped her instead and took her to his house. He started calling me and telling me to come and get her. I had a gut feeling that I shouldn't go, so I called the police. They said they couldn't do anything because he hadn't harmed her. He got my daughter to call; she was crying, and I could hear Bill in the background telling her to tell me to come and get her. Then he grabbed the phone and hit her in the face with it.

I called the police again and I got to Bills' house the same time they did. When I went into the house, there were guns and knives lined up on the kitchen table. He was planning on shooting me, and then cutting me up. Thank God I listened to my gut feeling.

I live with so many regrets, for myself and for my kids. I still get anxious when I'm gone from home very long. I feel like I need to hurry and get back. All I do is work and go home. I wasted so much of my life and for a man that was mean and selfish and cared about no one but himself. If I could say something to someone who was being abused, it would be: They won't change. Get out; get out while you still can. It never gets any better. Do whatever you have to in order to get out. It will get worse, and you'll be dead. That will be your end if you stay. Leave: the sooner the better.

I am not a has-been. I am a will be.
— Lauren Bacall

Women are like teabags.
We don't know our true strength until we are in hot water!
— Eleanor Roosevelt

A smile is the most beautiful curve on a woman's body.
— Author Unknown

Chapter 10

Pam's Story

Pam's story is different because it comes from a different angle. She told me about her mom, who was abused and eventually died due to the abuse. Ruth was sixty years old. Her first husband had passed away, and her second husband died nine months after they were married. Ruth was very depressed, so some of her friends got her to go to a shag-dancing club because they knew she enjoyed shagging. This is where she met David. David was a con artist but no one knew it at the time, especially Ruth. Two months after they started seeing each other, he convinced her to marry him and put his name on her bank accounts, her home. and her rental property. He took full control of her money. In a very short time, he made her cut all ties with her friends, family, and church members. He used her email account to send out letters, as if it were Ruth, to tell everyone she had someone in her life and not to contact her again. Pam was renting a mobile home from her mom, and David evicted her and sold the mobile home. Pam and her sister tried going to the police and Ruth's doctor, but nothing could be done because David was her spouse.

Can You See the Signs

This was not like their mom at all. A doctor told them that a person could be brainwashed in as little as three days. David put locks that only opened with a key on the windows, and put deadbolts that only opened with a key on the doors. Pam and her sister found out almost all the details after the fact. Pam and her sister weren't allowed to talk to their mom or see her. He would lock her in the house for days, sometimes in the closet. He beat her relentlessly. One time Pam went to the house and demanded to see her mom, and when Ruth came to the door, her eyes were black and her face was severely bruised. David said she had fallen. Pam and her sister made several attempts to get their mom out of that situation, but she was so afraid of him that she would always go back. David told Ruth that he would kill Pam if she didn't come back. Pam's sister was married, so he didn't mess with her.

Pam and her sister knew she was alive because the neighbors would see her. Pam and her sister would have bad dreams, and would wake up in the middle of the night and start praying for their mom. Neither one knew the other sister was having nightmares until they spoke the next day. It took eighteen months to get her completely free from this monster. During the last eight months, they were allowed no contact at all.

One morning Pam asked her coworkers to pray for her mom; most of them knew nothing about the abuse. Two hours later, Pam got a call to come and get her mom. It was a six-hour drive. When she got there her mom acted like she'd just seen Pam recently. Ruth was very confused. Pam asked her mom why the police took David to jail, and she said, " I don't know. They just came and took him." Pam said, "Mom, you know why they came and got him."

Pam's Story

Ruth had shut down mentally. Pam talked Ruth into giving her power of attorney. That helped Pam get her mom the help she needed, including a divorce from David. Pam and her sister took her to several doctors, psychiatrists, and neurologists to try and find out what to do for her. They found out that he had slammed her head into the walls of every room in the house. There were holes the size of her head in the sheetrock and blood splattered everywhere. David would try to smother her with a pillow when she was asleep. He choked her, beat her, and tried to drown her while she was in the bathtub. He broke her fingers but wouldn't let her go to the doctor. He kicked her, punched her, and knocked two of her teeth out. They finally found out she had traumatic brain injury from being beaten so much.

Pam was able to take care of Ruth for a year before she went into a rest home where she was comfortable and felt safe. She lived two years there. On her death certificate it said she died from head trauma due to the injuries she sustained years earlier. Ruth left six times but she'd always go back within three days because of the fear she had of that monster. If there is anything positive, it would be that during the last three years of her life, she couldn't remember anything but her two daughters.

Thank You

I WANT TO TAKE THE time to thank some of the people that had a big part in helping me through my domestic violence situation and that have helped make the vision of this book a reality.

Dr. Parsons, who for the twenty years I had her for my doctor was a big advocate against domestic violence. Thank you for your kindness and for never judging me. I miss you. Hope you're enjoying retirement.

Detective Rick Shelton, who for two years answered questions and helped me do everything according to the law to protect myself and my child. You are an angel here on earth.

To all the women at work who allowed me to hide change in their desks so I'd have some money to pay for a consultation with a lawyer. You guys are awesome. I love you all.

To my moma, who loved me through it all. Your prayers, your forgiveness, and your love are what helped me become the strong woman I am today. I wish everybody had a mom like you.

To my family and friends whose love and acts of kindness will be in my heart forever. Thank you!

To my husband, who is the most awesome man I've ever known. The Lord knew you were the only man that I would ever feel safe with and trust with my heart. Thank you for your love, your forgiveness, and for being willing to marry me twice. I am blessed beyond measure.

To my lil sis / best friend. God made us sisters but our boys and life made us best friends. I thank God for our relationship and for our love for each other. Thank you for seeing to it that this book became a reality. You knew where I wanted this book to go and you helped to get it there. Thanks for being the brains in this family. ☺

Last but far from least I want to thank all the prayer warriors out there who prayed for this book to get into print so it could impact others. God answered.

Thank you Lord for my happy heart.
I was broken and you healed my spirit.
— Proverbs 15:13.

A joyful heart makes a face cheerful, but a sad heart produces a broken spirit.

About the Author

My name is Denise Fenstermaker. I was born in California and raised in North Carolina. I guess you could say I'm a product of relocation. I'm a country girl but I love my jewelry. I love animals, trucks and motorcycles. I'm a member of the CMA (Christian Motorcyclists Association). I love being outdoors and being near water seems to be the best stress reliever ever. I like physical work, digging in the yard or creating new projects. I'm also an Avon Representative so I try not to do anything without my makeup on. My family is vitally important to me. I wouldn't be who I am today without their love and support. They help keep me grounded and sane. My son is my heart outside my body and my husband is my calming factor. I love to laugh and between my family and friends we do a lot of it. Laughter is the best medicine. Family motto: *That's okay, we'll do something else.* This saying has gotten us through more tough times than you can imagine. We just keep going. My favorite book is my Bible. I'd be lost without it.

I've experienced several forms of domestic violence in my life so I can relate to just about anyone who has been through it. It was about ten years ago that God gave me the vision of the book *Can You See the Signs*. To be honest I thought He was talking to the wrong person. I'm not a writer, I thought. The book is now complete and I hope and pray that it will benefit every person that reads it.

www.ingramcontent.com/pod-product-compliance
Lightning Source LLC
Chambersburg PA
CBHW052106070526
44584CB00017B/2361